I Am Awesome

Contents

Written by Poppy O'Neill

Collins

1 What is self-esteem?

Self-esteem is how you feel about yourself. When you have strong self-esteem, you feel good, hopeful and confident; with lower self-esteem, however, you can feel bad, negative and unhappy about yourself.

Everyone feels down some of the time – perhaps you do if you get embarrassed, you don't have a friend to sit with or you're faced with a challenge. A person with strong self-esteem is more able to be kind to themselves when they're feeling like this, because they believe they are a good person who can cope with difficult things.

When someone with lower self-esteem feels down about themselves, it's harder for them to treat themselves with kindness because lower self-esteem makes them believe they're not as good as other people.

Fact!

Your self-esteem can go up and down, depending on what's happening, your **emotions**, memories and how your body feels.

3

2 Why do we have self-esteem?

As human beings, we have **evolved** to live together in groups, families and communities. Because of this, our brains spend a lot of time working out how to fit in with the people around us.

Thousands of years ago, if you were an outsider to the group of people you lived with, you might not have got enough food to eat or a safe place to sleep. Our brains evolved to keep us safe from these dangers, and they still work in this way, even though our lives are very different now.

Fitting in is useful, and it's good to have some things in common with those around you, but it's also important to be yourself, even when that means you're different to your friends. Lower self-esteem can make us feel like fitting in is more important than being ourselves. Strong self-esteem can help us get the balance right between being ourselves and fitting in.

How do you feel about yourself?

You are the expert on how you feel about yourself. Ask yourself these questions to see if you have strong self-esteem:

- Do you feel mostly hopeful about the future?
- Do you like to try new things?
- Do you find it easy to stand up for yourself?
- When something is tricky, do you keep trying?
- When your friend does well, do you feel happy for them?

If the answer is "yes" to most or all of these questions, that's a sign of strong self-esteem. If you've answered "no" to most or all of the questions, that's a sign of lower self-esteem. Whichever way you've answered is OK and most people have self-esteem that's somewhere in the middle.

Fact!

It's impossible to feel 100% good about yourself all of the time. The trick is to find a way to be kind to yourself, however you're feeling.

7

Strong self-esteem is about feeling confident to be yourself, while letting other people be themselves too.

Our brains take in messages from the people around us.

This is Kara. She's learning to play the guitar and is really passionate about music. If Kara plays a song on her guitar and the people around her enjoy it, Kara's brain learns that playing the guitar helps her fit in and it feels good to play in front of people. But if she plays her guitar and the people around her don't like it, and tell her to stop, Kara's brain learns that playing her guitar feels bad and stops her from fitting in.

If Kara has strong self-esteem, she'll be more likely to notice that her friends were trying to concentrate on something else. She'll know that it's OK for her to play the guitar, but to consider those around her too. If she has lower self-esteem, she might think that her playing is bad, and that she should give up learning the guitar.

3 What boosts self-esteem?

For some people, boosting self-esteem takes practice. There are plenty of quick ways to boost your self-esteem, helping you feel confident and positive.

Here are a few ideas:

Strike a pose

Reach up tall and raise your chin. This tricks your brain and body into thinking and feeling confident.

Take a deep breath

Long, slow breaths calm your body – when you feel calmer, you feel automatically better about yourself.

Think about others

Considering how those around you might be feeling takes the focus and pressure off yourself.

Be honest

If you're feeling nervous or embarrassed, it's OK to say so! Naming your feelings makes them easier to manage.

Get together

Being with people you love and having fun makes you feel good!

Fact!

When we feel safe and confident, we breathe deeper, stand or sit up taller, speak honestly and enjoy being with others. So even if we're not feeling great, scientists believe that doing these things sends a signal from the body through the **vagus nerve** to the brain that it's OK to relax and act with confidence.

11

4 What is "self-talk"?

Self-talk is the voice you use to talk to and about yourself. Just like when you talk to someone else, self-talk can be respectful or disrespectful, kind or unkind. Self-talk is like having a little person following you around all the time. If your little self-talk person is kind, that helps boost your self-esteem. If it's unkind, it'll bring your self-esteem down.

Noticing when you use negative self-talk is one of the first steps to growing your self-esteem.

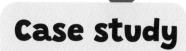

This is Jack, and he's having trouble with his Maths homework.

Jack thinks, *I'm so stupid! Why can't I understand this? Everybody else gets it – I'm just useless.*

Does this sound like positive or negative self-talk?

That's right – it's negative.

Jack realises that he's using negative self-talk. He thinks of something more positive to say to himself:

This is really hard! I need help to understand this. It's OK for me to ask for help when I need it.

Choosing kinder, more positive self-talk is one step towards stronger self-esteem. Just like understanding a new maths idea or learning a musical instrument, our brains need practice and encouragement to get better at positive self-talk.

It's OK that Jack's first thought was a negative one. The important thing is that he noticed, then chose a more positive thought – one that raised his self-esteem instead of bringing it down. It's about being your own best friend – it's useful to think, *Would I talk to a friend like this?* If you wouldn't, then don't talk to yourself that way!

I'm trying my best.

I'm learning all the time.

It makes sense that I feel this way.

Fact!
The more you practise positive self-talk, the more natural it will feel for your brain to think positively!

14

Here are some positive thoughts you might like to use next time you notice yourself using negative self-talk:

I can try again.

I'm not alone.

I can ask for help.

It's OK to be me.

I can talk about my worries.

My feelings matter.

5 What brings self-esteem down?

There are lots of things that can knock your self-esteem. Everyone has ups and downs with how they feel about themselves, and things like making a mistake, doing things that make you feel embarrassed or things not going your way can make you feel really bad about yourself for a while.

Being able to come back to feeling OK about yourself after a knock to your self-esteem can help us build **resilience**. It's important to be extra kind to yourself when something makes you feel bad about yourself.

Fact!

It's OK to find things difficult and need support. Some things that bring down your self-esteem are harder to deal with.

Things like:
- being bullied
- losing friends
- starting a new school

No matter what you're going through, you can always ask a **trusted adult** to help you understand and manage your emotions. You don't have to face difficult things alone.

6 Taking care of yourself

When you take care of your body, your self-esteem goes up! That's because when you've had enough to eat and drink and a good night's sleep, you're more able to think positively and feel good about yourself.

When our bodies don't feel good – when we're in pain, hungry, thirsty or tired – our brains are concerned with solving these problems. In order to build strong self-esteem, it's important to make sure our bodies have all the things we need, so our brains can relax.

Practising sport is a brilliant way to boost self-esteem because:

- your brain releases special chemicals called **endorphins** that make you feel happy and confident
- practising brings progress, which boosts self-esteem
- learning from mistakes builds your resilience
- emotions are expressed not just through words, but in the way we move, so exercise is a fantastic way to let our feelings show!

What makes *you* feel good? Taking time to do the things we enjoy is a big part of growing self-esteem. Doing something creative is great for self-esteem because making something new gives you opportunities to experiment, learn from mistakes and feel proud of your achievements.

Here are some creative activities that boost self-esteem:

- coding
- making art
- writing stories and poems
- dancing
- building models
- playing pretend

7 All feelings are OK

Strong self-esteem comes from accepting yourself, no matter what. This can be hard to do sometimes, especially when you're feeling a big emotion like anger, fear or embarrassment.

It's OK to feel any emotion. It's not OK to hurt others, and sometimes big emotions can make us want to do that. Your emotions belong to you, and being kind to your emotions is part of having strong self-esteem.

When you are kind and brave in the face of big emotions, they don't last very long – about one and a half minutes, according to scientists. Here's how to deal with big emotions:

1. Notice what you are feeling and give it a name – anger, fear, embarrassment, sadness … Remember that you are safe to feel this emotion.

2. Take a deep breath in, and slowly let it out. Keep breathing slowly and deeply until the emotion feels smaller and easier to manage.

When you know that you can deal with any emotion, your self-esteem grows stronger.

Remember!

You can always ask a friend or trusted adult to help you!

23

8 Building strong self-esteem

Growing your self-esteem takes practice and dedication. You're awesome exactly as you are, and helping your brain remember your awesomeness is the key to building strong self-esteem.

There's no quick way to building strong self-esteem, but you can use the ideas on pages 16 to 21 when you need a boost of confidence to help you stay kind to yourself, brave and positive.

If you're …

- practising positive self-talk
- asking for help when you need it
- treating your feelings with kindness

… then you're doing a great job of building up your self-esteem. It's a good idea to talk about self-esteem with a trusted adult – having someone who understands and is on your side is a brilliant self-esteem booster.

Fact!

Having strong self-esteem doesn't mean believing that you're perfect – it means knowing that nobody is perfect, being kind to yourself and learning from mistakes. Being kind to yourself even when it's difficult is when you're at your most awesome.

9 How to improve your self-esteem

Living with strong self-esteem is slightly different for everybody. It involves being kind to yourself, while also considering the feelings of others.

Here are a few ways you can practise building your self-esteem every day:

- speak up when something's not right for you
- say "yes" to challenges and opportunities
- ask for help when you need it
- stand up for yourself and your friends.

Some of these might be tricky, and it can feel quite scary to start acting with strong self-esteem if you're not used to it. As long as you're honest and respectful, it's OK to say things that others might not enjoy hearing.

Fact!

Growing your self-esteem is
a brave thing. When you act
with kindness and bravery, you
inspire others to do the same.
Remember your awesomeness
every day and your self-esteem
will grow and grow.

Glossary

emotions strong feelings arising from thoughts
 and experiences

endorphins chemicals sent from the brain to the body
 that make us feel happy

evolved Living things (including humans) change
 over many hundreds of years to better suit their
 environments. This is called evolution.

nerve a fibre in the body that carries messages and
 sensations to and from the brain

resilience the ability to feel OK again after difficulties

trusted adult a grown-up that you know and feel
 comfortable talking to about your feelings

vagus nerve the nerve which controls mood and carries
 messages between the brain and the heart, lungs
 and digestive system

Index

How will you grow your self-esteem?

Ideas for reading

Written by Christine Whitney
Primary Literacy Consultant

Reading objectives:
- identify and discuss themes in a wide range of writing
- retrieve, record and present information from non-fiction
- explain the meaning of words in context
- identify main ideas drawn from more than one paragraph and summarise these

Spoken language objectives:
- participate in discussion
- speculate, hypothesise, imagine and explore ideas through talk
- ask relevant questions

Curriculum links: Science: Animals, including humans: recognise the impact of diet, exercise, drugs and lifestyle on the way bodies function

Interest words: awesome, self-esteem, emotions, resilience

Resources: dictionaries

Build a context for reading
- Read the title of the book. Ask children to discuss the meaning of the word *awesome*.
- Ask children to use a dictionary to define the original meaning of this word. How is it used in the title of this book?
- What are children expecting to find inside the book? What might the different chapters be about?

Understand and apply reading strategies
- Read the contents page together. Was this what children expected? Ask them to explain what they think *self-esteem* means before they read Chapter 1.
- Continue to read together up to the end of Chapter 2. Ask children to summarise the difference between strong and lower self-esteem.
- Read independently up to the end of Chapter 4. What do they now know about *positive self-talk*?